TRADITIONAL STYLE KITCHENS

MODERN DESIGNS INSPIRED BY THE PAST

Melissa Cardona

Schiffer Publishing Ltd

4880 Lower Valley Road, Atglen, PA 19310 USA

Photography Credits

Front Cover: *Courtesy of Crown Point Cabinetry, Crystal Cabinet Works, and Quality Custom Cabinetry*
Page 1: *Courtesy of Küche + Cucina*
Page 2: *Courtesy of Crown Point Cabinetry*
Page 3: *Courtesy of Sroka Design, Inc., Knudsen Woodworking, Evelyn Benatar Interior Design, Cabinets Plus, Küche + Cucina, and Crystal Cabinet Works*
Back Cover: *Courtesy of Starmark Cabinetry*

Library of Congress Cataloging-in-Publication Data
Cardona, Melissa.
  Traditional style kitchens : modern designs inspired by the past / Melissa Cardona.
      p. cm.
  ISBN 0-7643-2285-0 (pbk.)
1. Kitchens. 2. Interior decoration. I. Title.

  NK2117.K5C37 2005
  747.7'97—dc22

                        2005007643

Designed by "Sue"
Type set in Carleton/American Garamand BT
ISBN: 0-7643-2285-0
Printed in China

Published by Schiffer Publishing Ltd.
4880 Lower Valley Road
Atglen, PA 19310
Phone: (610) 593-1777; Fax: (610) 593-2002
E-mail: Info@schifferbooks.com

For the largest selection of fine reference books on this and related subjects, please visit our web site at
www.schifferbooks.com
We are always looking for people to write books on new and related subjects. If you have an idea for a book please contact us at the above address.

This book may be purchased from the publisher.
Include $3.95 for shipping.
Please try your bookstore first.
You may write for a free catalog.

In Europe, Schiffer books are distributed by
Bushwood Books
6 Marksbury Ave.
Kew Gardens
Surrey TW9 4JF England
Phone: 44 (0) 20 8392-8585; Fax: 44 (0) 20 8392-9876
E-mail: info@bushwoodbooks.co.uk
Free postage in the U.K., Europe; air mail at cost.

CONTENTS

INTRODUCTION

The kitchen is the spiritual and functional center of the home, where the family congregates daily for meals, to do homework, pay bills, entertain guests, and just to sit and talk. Homeowners want their kitchens to support their lifestyles, and they are spending the money to make them do just that. Kitchens should be comfortable, with plenty of convenient and functional design features and the best in modern appliances. In addition to the functional aspects, the kitchen should also retain a style that harmonizes with the home's overall character and reflects the personality of the homeowners.

In this book, are images of traditional style kitchens for homeowners who want a state-of-the-art kitchen with timeless appeal. These amazing rooms were meticulously designed by some of the most talented kitchen designers working today. At the heart of these designs is cabinetry – which represents the biggest expense in kitchen projects. You will see why in the kitchens featured here. Cabinetry sets the tone for the kitchen's style, establishing the room's personality and ambience. Fine craftsmanship, architectural detailing, beautiful finishes, and furniture-like designs are just some of the features you'll see in these traditional kitchens.

Authentic period style kitchens to transitional designs, casual farmhouse kitchens to elegant and formal styles are featured in this book. Each kitchen has been infused with details that will inspire you and the look of your kitchen. A resource guide in the back of the book includes a list of kitchen designers, cabinetry manufacturers, and other contributors that will help you in your quest for your own traditonal style kitchen.

PERIOD KITCHENS

A historic home's kitchen is a study in handcrafted beauty and simplicity. Only the bare essentials are found in this kitchen, but green cabinetry in a classic 18th century style, a walnut island, and reclaimed timber beams create interest in a space that's in keeping with the home's architectural styling. The top of the refrigerator features a slatted design for ventilation reminiscent of Livery Style, a pattern that is continued on the doorways throughout the home. The homeowners wanted the island to give the impression of having been added to the kitchen's design, thus giving the room a sense of continuity. *Courtesy Knudsen Woodworking*

Glass-fronted cabinets topped by
windows characterize this kitchen,
which complements a historic
home's personality. The use of
reproduction style hardware and
stucco walls are additional
distinguishing features. The
refrigerator and freezer were
disguised with a furniture-like
cabinet in a distressed red finish.
Courtesy of Blue Bell Kitchens

Photography by Bruce Van Inwegan

The home's original laundry room was converted into a walk-in pantry with abundant storage space and concealed laundry appliances, allowing for the use of glass-fronted cabinets in the kitchen. Antique hardware and beadboard detailing accent the beautiful custom cabinetry. A custom hood, stovetop backsplash, and butcher-block island extension complete the space, creating a kitchen full of beauty and utility. *Courtesy of Quality Custom Cabinetry, www.qcc.com, and Past Basket, Inc. / Design by Dan McFadden and Jennifer McKnight*

Combining multiple colors and textures creates a warm atmosphere in this farmhouse kitchen. Extensive storage space was made available with the installation of plenty of large cabinets, and a historical look was maintained with appliances hidden behind cabinet doors. Wide plank floors, exposed beams, and a mix of countertop materials complete the look. *Courtesy of Quality Custom Cabinetry, www.qcc.com, Nettesheim's Classic Kitchens & Designs, and Bon Marche Interiors / Design by Mark Nettesheim, CKD and Elaine Hall Murray, CKD, Allied Member ASID*

The beauty of this Craftsman-style cabinetry is found in simple geometric lines, exquisite dark wood, mission toekicks, and period-style hardware. A white apron sink complements the reproduction-style stove, and a green tile backsplash punctuates the space with color. A hammered copper hood glitters under recessed spotlights, adding polish to a kitchen rich in matte finishes.
Courtesy of Crown Point Cabinetry

The owner of this home wanted the kitchen to reflect her sense of style yet remain appropriate for her 1940s colonial style home. The desired effect was achieved by using a custom finish on the cabinetry, weathered copper countertops, reproduction faucets, and slate tile flooring. The cook center's wood countertops provide a convenient surface for the cook, while also providing contrast and texture. *Courtesy of Quality Custom Cabinetry, www.qcc.com, www.qcc.com and Past Basket, Inc. / Design by Dave McFadden and Jennifer McKnight*

~

Photography by Larry Fields

Photography by Joseph Korona

An Arts and Crafts style kitchen (shown here and on the following 3 pages) radiates warmth with the use of wood. Custom cabinetry was built to look like separate pieces of furniture, giving a cozy, lived-in feel to the kitchen. Tiled in stone, the stovetop backsplash continues along the length of wall, boasting four decorative shelves and contrasting beautifully with purple cabinetry. *Courtesy of Quality Custom Cabinetry, www.qcc.com, and Kitchen & Bath Concepts / Design by Tom Trzcinski, CMKBD*

This farmhouse kitchen opens into the adjacent keeping room and foyer, where it is visible immediately upon entering the home. Natural materials complement the rest of the home's restored interior – natural and stained cherry pieces are combined with granite and wood countertops for an authentic, rustic look. All the appliances are concealed because of the kitchen's visibility. Rather than conventional cabinetry, the kitchen is fitted with furniture-like workstations for a truly vintage feel. *Courtesy of YesterTec*

Photography by Hub Willson

Dennis Degnan Photography

Glass-fronted display cabinets maintain the open, airy quality established by the kitchen's large windows. Window treatments and gorgeous handcrafted cabinetry give a feeling of permanence and luxury. The cabinetry and island were handcrafted in the classic 18th century style. The walnut island and flooring add warmth to the room. *Courtesy of Knudsen Woodworking*

~

Flooring made from old wood joists adds rustic flair and history to a kitchen with an elegant chandelier and handcrafted, 18th century style cabinets. The style for the butternut cabinetry was borrowed from a Long Island home built in 1906 and featured in the film *North by Northwest*. *Courtesy of Knudsen Woodworking*

~

Blue and white country style cabinetry was paired with elegant marble countertops and stainless steel appliances for an eclectic look that fits the style of a 1700s stone house.
Courtesy of Kitchens By Design / Design by Catherine Hodgins

Photography by Gordon Beall

A custom finish on the kitchen cabinetry feigns the patina of age, a look made all the more authentic with the use of reproduction style fixtures and natural wood flooring. Natural light illuminates the island to create a desirable and well-lit workspace. *Courtesy of Sroka Design, Inc. / Design by Skip Sroka, ASID*

The slate-blue cabinetry in this cozy kitchen was finished in a nutmeg stain and painted with old-fashioned milk paint for an authentic early American look. Hardware with an aged patina, soapstone countertops, and farmhouse antique furniture also contribute to the space's authenticity. *Courtesy of Crown Point Cabinetry*

The simplicity of Shaker style cabinetry lends itself to both traditional and contemporary styling. Here, soapstone countertops and an apron sink establish a more traditional look. A pegboard above the sink provides a convenient option for hanging dishtowels, while the open shelves provide handy storage for frequently used china. *Courtesy of Quality Custom Cabinetry, www.qcc.com / Design by Harold Martin*

Soapstone countertops and olive-gray cabinetry establish the look of this colonial kitchen. A brick backdrop with recessed spotlight makes an attractive focal point in lieu of a hood. *Courtesy of Vermont Soapstone*

A collection of heirloom plates decorates the stovetop's backsplash, complementing the warm walnut hues of the kitchen's island and flooring. A truncated arch forms the room's focal point – the shape is set off by the island's arched corner panels. *Courtesy of Knudsen Woodworking*

This historic home's Shaker style cherry cabinetry is contrasted by a blue island and darker corner display cabinet. In a space with little ornamentation, darker trim and beadboard backsplashes go a long way to create interest. *Courtesy of Quality Custom Cabinetry, www.qcc.com/ Design by Fred Miller*

Accent tiles in the backsplash complement the olive-gray color of the kitchen's central island. Reproduction style light fixtures maintain the colonial styling established in the kitchen's color palette and cabinetry. *Courtesy of Signature Custom Cabinetry and Lobkovich Kitchen Designs / Design by J. Paul Lobkovich*

The owners of this historic home wanted their kitchen to reflect the home's architectural style. Modern appliances were hidden behind cabinet doors and paired with distressed finished cabinetry, reproduction style fixtures, wide plank flooring, and natural textures to achieve a historic look. The stove's mantel hood and backsplash create the expansive room's focal point, as well as a fruit theme continued in the wibdow treatments. *Courtesy of Blue Bell Kitchens*

The past is evoked with state of the art appliances crafted to look like antiques. The look of slate tile flooring, handcrafted cabinetry in a buttermilk yellow, and glass-fronted doors adds more ambiance. *Courtesy of Elmira Stove Works*

TRANSITIONAL KITCHENS

Photography by Bennett Mossé

The complete renovation of a colonial style home included the transformation of the originally dark and depressing kitchen. The space was designed to be a bright and cheerful gathering place for the family that retained the traditional elements of the home's architecture. The effect is a fresh and authentic design that remains true to the home's original style. *Courtesy of Evelyn Benatar Interior Design*
~

The welcoming, comfortable feeling of the nostalgic past is expressed in this kitchen's styling. Trim, rope moulding, and fluted columns on either side of the refrigerator provide a dramatic focal point in conjunction with a hutch on the opposite wall. A pewter glaze was used on the cabinetry to add an antiqued patina, complementing the historically inspired kitchen design. *Courtesy of Wood-Mode*

~

The owner of this 1914 Georgian Colonial Revival home wanted her out-of-date kitchen to reflect the home's traditional styling. Cabinetry with beaded panels and limestone countertops were chosen to provide the authentic look she desired. *Courtesy of Wood-Mode and The Kitchen Works / Design by Julie Vagts, ASID, CID*

Traditional styling gets an update with funky flair. Color adds life to this kitchen, where modern appliances meet traditional elements for a fun and versatile look. *Courtesy of Sroka Design, Inc. / Design by Skip Sroka, ASID*

Shaker style cabinets, with their clean and elegant lines, lend themselves to both traditional and contemporary styling. Here, sleek black granite countertops complement black appliances for a look that's simple and refined. *Courtesy of Crown Point Cabinetry*

Rich in details, this kitchen boasts an eclectic and attractive array of decorative features. Timber beams on the ceiling, painted finishes on the cabinetry, and unique window treatments all lend themselves to a rustic look. Two islands afford extra work and entertainment space while punctuating the room with color. A copper hood creates another focal point in the kitchen, complemented by hammered copper sinks. *Courtesy of Crown Point Cabinetry*
~

A stone wall provides the perfect backdrop for a farmhouse style kitchen. The cabinetry maintains traditional warmth while exuding a minimalist aesthetic for a dynamic, transitional look. *Courtesy of SieMatic*

~

Doubling as a pot rack, a distinctively designed light fixture hangs above one of two islands in this kitchen. The relationship of historic and modern styling creates a wonderful and attractive dynamic, with state of the art appliances hidden among handcrafted cabinetry. *Courtesy of Crown Point Cabinetry*

~

Features like corbels on the island, a plate rack with beaded back, paneled refrigerator, and dark wood floors establish a comfortable, traditional décor in this kitchen, which is carried over into the adjacent office and dining areas. *Courtesy of Fieldstone Cabinetry / Design by Jeff Ptacek, CKD*

~

MacNabb Photography

The backside of a kitchen's island is left free of cabinetry to accommodate seating. The cool hues of countertops and decorative backsplashes are warmed with a cherry island topped by a butcher-block countertop. Cabinetry in the kitchen's breakfast nook provides storage for tablecloths, napkins, and placemats, as well as glass-fronted display cabinets for interest. *Courtesy of Blue Bell Kitchens*

Past and present coexist harmoniously in this combination of stainless steel appliances and period style cabinetry. Small touches like light fixtures above the kitchen's two islands, a beadboard wall, and tiled backsplash add personality. Glass-fronted cabinets serve to open up the space, as does the original window left in the design of this kitchen addition. *Courtesy of Crown Point Cabinetry*

A bright kitchen takes advantage of the light with cabinetry painted in antique white. Silver maple and soapstone countertops add texture and a sense of history, while glass-fronted cabinets in the island contribute to the room's airiness. A narrow spice rack with a glass door was built into the wall for a unique and charming touch, and the drawer-style dishwasher was hidden among cabinetry for a stealthy approach to kitchen clean up. *Courtesy of Crown Point Cabinetry*

An island countertop adds warmth to the cool blue and gray hues of a historic home's kitchen. Creamy white beadboard and colonial blue cabinetry were paired to complement the home's historic personality, and light gray soapstone was chosen to set off stainless steel appliances. *Courtesy of Blue Bell Kitchens*

A black-and-white checkered pattern in the stove's backsplash creates the kitchen's focal point and is echoed in the island seating for continuity. The island's antiqued white finish adds contrast and interest to the simplicity of Shaker-style cabinetry. *Courtesy of Blue Bell Kitchens*

~

MacNabb Photography

Glass-fronted cabinetry was meticulously worked into the uneven ceiling of this 1700s home. Shelves were painted blue to match blue countertops, and cork flooring adds a natural, textured look to the room. *Courtesy of Kitchens By Design / Design by Catherine Hodgins*

~

Cool blue cabinetry is paired with farmhouse styling for a warm and cozy kitchen. Convenient metal rods hung in the beadboard backsplashes offer hooks to hang pots, pans, and random utensils. *Courtesy of SieMatic*

~

Clean white styling and distinctive detailing characterize this cozy cottage kitchen that breathes fresh life into country styling. Lots of open shelving and glass-fronted display cabinets keep the room open and airy. *Courtesy of SieMatic*

~

Copper brings warmth and shine to this country home's kitchen, where fine craftsmanship and attention to detail suggest permanence. Lights above the cabinetry expand the space, drawing attention upward, where stenciling adds interest.
Courtesy of Cabinets Plus / Design by Lou Nardolillo / Jeff Hallock Builder

Authentic artifacts from America's Southwest add décor to a kitchen dominated by Shaker-inspired cherry cabinetry. Reclaimed timber beams and beautiful wide plank flooring also celebrate the natural beauty of wood. *Courtesy of Knudsen Woodworking*

~

Above and Right: The kitchen island, beadboard backsplash, and a stack of drawers are stained with a darker finish to create interest among antiqued white cabinetry. Custom cabinet design allows for the inclusion of a nook next to the stove, where baskets slide in and out for easy retrieval of potatoes and onions. The hood features a display shelf for added décor and coziness. *Courtesy of Crown Point Cabinetry*

A wall of windows floods the kitchen with light, but eats up cabinet space. The lost storage is made up for with the inclusion of a large island and cabinets on the side of the refrigerator. Terracotta and wood countertops were paired to add texture, and Oriental rugs provide décor to a truly traditional style space. *Courtesy of Blue Bell Kitchens*

Yellow walls dress a kitchen in sunshine. Together with furniture style cherry cabinetry in a warm finish, they create an inviting atmosphere. Toile window treatments and decorative elements behind the stovetop add to the coziness. *Courtesy of Fieldstone Cabinetry / Design by Jeff Ptacek, CKD*

Distressed and rustic cabinetry finishes add authenticity to a modern-day farmhouse kitchen. In the modestly-sized room, the custom-painted island and matching cabinets seem to open up the space by providing contrast. *Courtesy of Quality Custom Cabinetry, www.qcc.com, and Nettesheim's Classic Kitchens & Designs / Design by Mark Nettesheim, CKD*

Left and below: Large glass doors flood the kitchen with light, but take up precious space that could have been used for cabinetry. To create storage, the vaulted ceiling was continued into a hood-like construction above the island to hang pots and pans, adding a decorative touch while maintaining the kitchen's historically inspired styling. *Courtesy of Plain & Fancy Custom Cabinetry*

Opposite page: Traditional country styling has a stately appearance in this kitchen, where copper surfaces and antiqued finishes combine for a historic look. The mantel hood design resembles those found in kitchens from colonial times. *Courtesy of Crystal Cabinet Works/Design by Helen Marshburn*

~

What happens when a farmhouse enters the 21st century? Here, stainless steel appliances add polish to a rustic-looking kitchen characterized by reclaimed beams and a red barn finish on the cabinetry. Glass-fronted cabinets, a display shelf, and mini drawers in a natural finish form the room's focal point. *Courtesy of Crystal Cabinet Works/ Design by Sarah Aldrich*

A traditional farmhouse kitchen was updated for the 21st century with state of the art appliances. The traditional look was preserved with exposed beams and custom beadboard panels. The kitchen's large island provides plenty of space for food prep, along with a warming drawer to keep food warm and fresh until dinnertime. Notice the backsplash of multi-paned windows, which soak the kitchen in natural light.
Courtesy of Jenn-Air

The use of contrasting colors and finishes has a strong visual impact in this unique kitchen. A custom finish on the kitchen's island and cook center was achieved with hand sanding and gives the impression of age. Beaded inset cabinets with exposed hinges accent the kitchen's traditional appeal, and granite countertops in stepped levels are a convenient feature for the cook. *Courtesy of Keener Kitchen Manufacturing / Design by Chris Jacobs, CKD*

This kitchen was customized to maintain a carriage house theme while modernizing the room's functionality. Sleek, modern appliances were paired with reclaimed hardwood floors and reproduction fixtures, creating a dynamic space full of character and charm. *Courtesy of BNK Design Consultants*

This bright country kitchen evokes memories of a simpler time. Although the glass doors, turned posts, wooden beams and mantel, as well as the plank flooring all had their origin in the American homestead era, they're right at home in today's kitchen with the latest appliances and convenience options. The pewter glaze creates an aged look that complements the period-style details. *Courtesy of Wood-Mode*

~

Photography by George Kopp

An antique table adds history to this kitchen and serves as the central island. Custom cabinetry features a distressed finish to complement the aged look of the original antique, while the stainless steel appliances and sink bring a bit of contemporary flash to the kitchen. *Courtesy of Signature Custom Cabinetry and Saw Horse Designs / Design by Tom McCloskey*

The use of three different painted finishes on selected pieces of cabinetry creates a cozy, collected atmosphere. Beaded inset cabinet doors and furniture-like toekicks add to traditional styling, which also includes the use of filigreed hardware and decorative brackets on the kitchen island. *Courtesy of Crown Point Cabinetry*

Photography by John Jenkins

The homeowner wanted to include an antique, hand-painted set of drawers in the design of this kitchen to give it a cozy, country look. Multiple finishes and countertop materials add to the collected look of the space, and custom cabinetry provides handcrafted details that give a sense of permanence.
Courtesy of Kitchens By Design / Design by Catherine Hodgins

Trompe L'oeil decorative painting brings life to this small kitchen, where an inoperable fire-place, breakfast nook, and multiple doors and windows leave little wall space for traditional cabinetry. Space-efficient workstations with old-time character hide appliances in a small amount of space. The cherry pieces feature painted perforated metal panels and granite countertops, and the soapstone sink was ground with a belt sander to give the appearance of age. *Courtesy of YesterTec and Bon FAUXnique*

The past is evoked in a modern kitchen with the help of reclaimed barn wood that was milled and installed as wide plank flooring. With so much space available, the homeowner placed an upholstered armchair at each end of the table for a truly relaxed approach to dining. *Courtesy of Aged Woods®/Yesteryear Floorworks Co. / Design by Binkley-Ford Assoc, Inc./Custom Millwork by C W Keller & Associates*

Soapstone provides a luxurious look and soft texture to this kitchen. The countertop and custom sink in a deep, rich gray are heat resistant, nonporous, virtually impossible to stain, and completely natural. With its unique properties, soapstone is well suited to traditional styles. *Courtesy of Vermont Soapstone*

Colored finishes were combined to create a warm, charming space. *Courtesy of Blue Bell Kitchens*

FORMAL KITCHENS

A kitchen with three separate islands deserves the addition of a coffered ceiling, luxurious window treatments, and a custom hood with limestone finish. Two arched cabinets flank the reproduction stove and custom hood to add interest, and various finishes on the cabinetry helps to distinguish different areas of the kitchen. *Courtesy of Küche + Cucina*

Rustic wood was chosen for the furniture-like cabinetry, rich with embellishments like moulding and inset doors. The highlight of this kitchen can be found around the stove, inset into the wall and adorned with a tile backsplash and wood moulding. Lights were used as a decorative feature here, too, glowing inside display cabinets, overhead in recessed fixtures, and even below the island's countertop. *Courtesy of Canyon Creek Cabinet Company*

Furniture-style cabinetry featuring a rich antique finish with butterscotch highlights gives a luxurious atmosphere to this kitchen. Attention is drawn to the kitchen's cherry island, with its green granite countertop and darker finish. Cabinet hardware in fruit and vegetable shapes adds a charming touch. *Courtesy of Crystal Cabinet Works / Design by Katrina Shirk*

A magnificently lavish kitchen is embellished with rich details in the cabinetry, tile backsplashes, light fixtures, and antique furnishings. An expansive island provides contrast with its dark countertop and finish, which are complemented by the stovetop backsplash and light fixtures. Stainless steel appliances, with their clean styling, complement the kitchen's traditional appeal. *Courtesy of Jenn-Air*

Photography by Doug Edmonds

Open storage space underneath the stove makes for easy access to pots and pans, and a spice cabinet with a glass-fronted door is conveniently placed next to the cook's command center. A paneled backsplash behind the cooktop, in combination with the large mantle hood, gives the stove area a furniture-like character. *Courtesy of Crystal Cabinet Works/Design by Tove Kenyon*

Display spaces and window treatments add personality to the kitchen. With cabinetry built up to the ceiling, the mantel hood's display shelf offers a break in the continuity and a point of interest. *Courtesy of Plain & Fancy Custom Cabinetry*

A brick surround houses this kitchen's stove and classic 18th century cabinetry, adding texture and a focal point to the room. *Courtesy of Knudsen Woodworking*

~

Yellow walls help to brighten a room rich in dark wood tones, while windows lining the ceiling allow for the inclusion of ample cabinetry and light. The island features a unique, three-piece tiered design, leading the eye to the room's focal point: the hood and stovetop backsplash, which is repeated behind the sink. *Courtesy of Merillat*

~

The combination of creamy white and natural wood finishes on the cabinetry is pulled together with the use of the black accent display cabinet, pulls, corbels, and the island countertop. Rich, moulded detailing adds luxury to the kitchen, where custom cabinet design creates convenient, one-of-a-kind options for storage. *Courtesy of Quality Custom Cabinetry, www.qcc.com, www.qcc.com / Design by Harold Martin*

~

An expansive kitchen was made cozy through the use of different door styles. Corbels and a chocolate glaze add history to the modern space. An island countertop was extended to include bar-top seating for a casual meal, or a place for guests to gather as the hosts make preparations in the designated workspaces. *Courtesy of Canyon Creek Cabinet Company*

Photography by Doug Edmonds

Cabinetry was consolidated on one side of a galley kitchen, leaving the other side free for large, space-expanding windows. A window and door were included at the end of the kitchen to open up the space even more, and wallpaper was chosen to add color and drama. *Courtesy of Crystal Cabinet Works/Design by Tove Kenyon*

Tiled backsplashes bring together colorful accents throughout this farmhouse kitchen. The deep green island and paneled refrigerator contrast beautifully with red walls and a reproduction style stove and oven. Reclaimed timber beams add a rustic touch to the lavishness of furniture-quality cabinetry, in conjunction with decorative country style accents. The overall effect is a cozy kitchen – rich in detail and personality. *Courtesy of Quality Custom Cabinetry, www.qcc.com, www.qcc.com / Design by Harold Martin*

Photography by Dale Quarterman

Above: Two glass-fronted display cabinets flank an arched mantle hood and show off colorful ceramics and glassware. An ornate chandelier above the island adds luxury to the space, rich in warmth and cozy ambience. *Courtesy of Crystal Cabinet Works/Design by Abigail Bishop*

Right: Farmhouse and kitchen antiques add décor and history to an elegant, traditionally styled kitchen. The workstation was left open to the eating nook and dining room to maintain the airiness provided by large windows. *Courtesy of Kitchens By Design / Design by Catherine Hodgins*

Photography by John Jenkins

Brick was used to create a warm, inviting, arched hood area, with convenient "Pot Filler" faucet and professional range below. Storage cabinets to house condiments, spices, and other cooking necessities flank the brick hood. Brick was also used in the adjacent alcove to accommodate the microwave and unique storage area, featuring pull-out wicker baskets for linen storage. Notice the use of formal traditional Georgian pediments and fluted pilasters surrounding the microwave alcove and the built-in refrigerator. These custom cabinetry features give the kitchen a sense of regency and elegance, complemented by the strong warmth of brick stonework. *Courtesy of Signature Custom Cabinetry and Bella Cucina, Inc. / Design by Jeana Morrison, CKD*

Red accent walls complement red cabinet doors and give added depth to this kitchen. The island's custom-finished beadboard in conjunction with cream and red cabinetry lends a collected look. Featuring all the best in modern design and appliances, historically inspired styling speaks of permanence and tradition. *Courtesy of Signature Custom Cabinetry and Bailey Avenue Kitchens / Design by Judi Stoogenke, ASID*

~

Tinted varnish, glazing, and distressing give cabinetry the look of age. Rope moulding, corbels, pewter hardware, beaded end panels, and textured glass-door insets add luxury to the old-fashioned look. A bar-top eating area is made from copper to complement the copper hood. Panels cover up unattractive appliances, while glass-fronted display cabinets are fashioned with lights for added décor. *Courtesy of StarMark Cabinetry*

A U-shaped layout proves quite convenient to this kitchen's cook, who loves to entertain. Bar-top seating is provided with the extension and elevation of the sink's countertop area, saving space and creating distinct zones within the kitchen. The custom hearth perimeter is cherry with a glaze, while the island features a contrasting paint with glaze and sandthrough. *Courtesy of Signature Custom Cabinetry / Design by Richard Rotunda*

~

The stove was placed cattycorner to create a more functional and attractive layout. As such, the mantle hood and black stove serve as a focal point in this detail-rich kitchen. The island's walnut countertop provides contrast among more neutral, subdued tones, while the window treatment above the sink complements the gold-painted walls. *Courtesy of Signature Custom Cabinetry and Bailey Avenue Kitchens*

~

Architectural accents distinguish these pine wood cabinets in a natural finish. Pierced filigree, reeded pilasters, hand carved panels, custom turned posts, and a variety of mouldings add luxury to this design, which also features black granite countertops and a white farmhouse sink. The kitchen island, with its unique furniture-like design, provides multiple storage options for large and small kitchen items. *Courtesy of Quality Custom Cabinetry, www.qcc.com and Cox Kitchens & Baths / Design by Allison Gibbs, CKD*

An island and a peninsula were included in the design of this kitchen to provide convenient workspaces in a room with a long layout. The neutral tones of the cabinetry and flooring are punctuated with a colorful stovetop backsplash, which acts as the area's focal point in coordination with the similarly shaped window. *Courtesy of Küche + Cucina*

Photography by John Jenkins

Opposite page, top: A cherry island topped with blue granite is the main attraction of this kitchen. The island's lower level features a semi-circular extension perfect for more casual meals. Spacious and refined, this kitchen blends in seamlessly with the home's formal décor. *Courtesy of Kitchens By Design / Design by Catherine Hodgins*

Opposite page, bottom: Birch cabinets with a toffee stain and antique glaze were combined with oak flooring and a stone veneer cooking alcove to create a traditional look. Antique pewter birdcage pulls and knobs were chosen to adorn the cabinets and complement the kitchen's stainless steel appliances and sinks. The island's solid oak topper coordinates with the oak flooring and a herringbone pattern tumbled marble backsplash creates interest. Custom built doors that were painted and glazed to match the cabinetry houses a baking center. *Courtesy of Keener Kitchen Manufacturing / Design by Chris Jacobs, CKD*

MacNabb Photography

This home's galley kitchen is the cook center as well as a cozy nook for relaxation. A large window was included at the head of the room to open up the room, and offers space for a window seat and an armchair. An antique butcher block table provided the inspiration for the cabinetry, and a tabletop extension provides dining space for two. *Courtesy of Blue Bell Kitchens*

Glass-fronted display cabinets flank a window to create a point of interest in the kitchen. The stovetop backsplash stretches along the length of the countertop, adding contrast to the space with darker diamond tiles. *Courtesy of Signature Custom Cabinetry and Bailey Avenue Kitchens / Design by Judi Stoogenke, ASID*

Birch cabinets in a rich brown hue, with their open shelves, beaded inset, and spindle post accents add décor to an otherwise austere kitchen. The painted and distressed island is topped with a custom-made maple top to contrast with the darker pantry and wall cabinets and the Corian countertops in a neutral linen color. *Courtesy of Keener Kitchen Manufacturing / Design by Chris Jacobs, CKD*

The limited space of a kitchen prep area was maximized by including a large palladian window flanked by two glass-fronted display cabinets. Beautiful mouldings on the cabinetry carry the warmth of the adjacent dining area into the kitchen and maintain the home's traditional styling. Tiled backsplashes establish a country theme while adding color to the space. *Courtesy of Quality Custom Cabinetry, www.qcc.com, and Riverside Custom Design / Design by Gene Pindzia*

Elegance and modern convenience are combined with tradition in a kitchen fit for a royal family. Neo-classical columns make a dramatic transition into the kitchen, where appliances have been covered by cabinet doors and a reproduction style stove was included to keep with the traditional look. *Courtesy of Küche + Cucina*

RESOURCES

Aged Woods®/Yesteryear
    Floorworks Co.
York, PA
(800) 233-9307
www.agedwoods.com
Page 80

BNK Design Consultants
West Conshohocken, PA
(610) 941-2943
www.bnkdesign.com
Pages 68-69

Bailey Avenue Kitchens
Ridgefield, CT
(203) 438-4868
www.baileyavenuekitchens.com
Page 97, 101, 108

Bella Cucina, Inc.
Orlando, FL
(407) 228-9823
www.bellacucinainc.com
Page 96

Blue Bell Kitchens
Springhouse, PA
(215) 646-5442
www.bluebellkitchens.com
Pages 7, 29, 44, 48, 49, 57, 81, 107

Bon FAUXnique
Kempton, PA
(610) 285-6536
www.bonfauxnique.com
Pages 78-79

Bon Marche Interiors
Brisbane, CA
(650) 340-1138
Pages 10-11

Cabinets Plus
Riverhead, NY
(631) 727-8062
www.cabinetsplusny.com
Pages 52-53

Canyon Creek Cabinet Company
(800) 228-1830
www.canyoncreek.com
Pages 84, 92-93

Cox Kitchens & Baths, Inc.
Baltimore, MD
(410) 296-4700
www.coxkitchensandbaths.com
Pages 102-103

Crown Point Cabinetry
Claremont, NH
(800) 999-4994
www.crown-point.com
Pages 2, 12-13, 25, 39, 40, 41, 45, 46-47, 56,
74-75

Crystal Cabinet Works
Princeton, MN
(800) 347-5045
www.ccworks.com
Pages 63, 64-65, 85, 87, 94, 95

Elmira Stove Works
(800) 295-8498
www.elmirastoveworks.com
Pages 30-31

Evelyn Benatar Interior Design
Great Neck, NY
(516) 482-4787
www.nyinteriordesign.com
Pages 32-33

Fieldstone Cabinetry
(800) 339-5369
www.fieldstonecabinetry.com
Pages 42-43, 58-59

Jeff Hallock Builders
Jamesport, NY
(631) 722-3261
Pages 52-53

Jenn-Air
(800) JENN-AIR
www.jennair.com
Pages 66, 86

Keener Kitchen Manufacturing
(717) 244-4544
www.keenerkitchen.com
Pages 67, 106, 108

Kitchen & Bath Concepts
Pittsburgh, PA
(412) 369-2900
www.kitchenbathconceptspittsburgh.com
Pages 16-19

Kitchen Works
Pasadena, CA
(626) 405-1926
Pages 36-37

Kitchens By Design
Wilmington, DE
(302) 529-7015
www.kbdinc.com
Pages 24, 50, 76-77, 95, 106

Knudsen Woodworking
Kirkwood, PA
(717) 529-4011
www.knudsenwoodworking.com
Pages 6, 22, 23, 27, 54-55, 90

Küche + Cucina
Paramus, NJ
(201) 261-5221
www.kuche-cucina.com
Pages 1, 82-83, 104-105, 110-111

Lobkovich Kitchen Designs
Tysons Corner, VA
(703) 847-0601
www.lobkovich.com
Page 28

Merillat
(517) 263-0771
www.merillat.com
Page 90

Nettesheim's Classic Kitchens
    & Designs
Carmel, CA
(831) 622-9260
www.classickitchens.us
Pages 10-11, 60-61

Past Basket, Inc.
Geneva, IL
(630) 208-1011
www.pastbasket.com
Pages 8-9, 14-15

Plain & Fancy Custom Cabinetry
(717) 949-6571
www.plainfancycabinetry.com
Pages 62, 88-89

Quality Custom Cabinetry
(800) 909-6006
www.qcc.com
Pages 8-9, 10-11, 14-15, 16-18, 26, 28, 60-61,
91, 94, 102-103, 109

Richard Rotunda
Millburn, NJ
(973) 912-4440
www.kitchenexpressions.com
Page 100

Riverside Custom Design
Grosse Pointe Woods, MI
(313) 886-3188
www.riversidecustom.com
Page 109

SieMatic
(800) 765-5266
www.siematic.com
Pages 41, 51

Signature Custom Cabinetry, Inc.
(717) 738-6981
www.signaturecab.com
Pages 28, 72-73, 96, 97, 100, 101-108

Saw Horse Designs
Millburn, NJ
(973) 376-5700
www.sawhorsedesigns.com
Pages 72-73

Sroka Design, Inc.
Bethesda, MD
(301) 263-9100
www.srokadesign.com
Pages 4-5, 25, 38

StarMark Cabinetry
(800) 594-9444
www.starmarkcabinetry.com
Pages 98-99

Vermont Soapstone
(802) 263-5404
www.vermontsoapstone.com
Page 27, 80

Wood-Mode
(877) 635-7500
www.wood-mode.com
Pages 34-35, 36-37, 70-71

YesterTec Design Company
Center Valley, PA
(877) 346-4976
www.yestertec.com
Pages 20-21, 78-79